HOW TO GO TO THE POORHOUSE --- FIRST CLASS!

HOW TO GO TO THE POORHOUSE --- FIRST CLASS!

By

Daria

Copyright © 1999 by Daria

All rights reserved. No part of this book may be reproduced, stored in a retrieval system, or transmitted by any means, electronic, mechanical, photocopying, recording, or otherwise, without written permission from the author.

ISBN: 1-58500-851-6

1stbooks - rev.01/27/00

About the Book

The book contains practical strategies for surviving financial disasters. It draws on illustrations of Europeans and Americans who have handled the barbs of fate with style, and come out on top. It suggests ways to maximize whatever is left in the till, and hopes to remind the reader that he has not suffered any lasting damage--it is only his bank account that has been diminished. Self esteem must never be linked to possessions. Often what appears to be bad luck is the stepping-stone to personal growth.....and ATTITUDE is all important

Gentle Reader

One can only assume that if you have rushed out to buy this book your financial affairs are suddenly in a precarious state and that certain adjustments must be immediately made. The book is purposely quite thin; first, to serve as a reminder not to indulge in compensatory eating, and second, to save you the price of a larger volume---paper costs you know, to say nothing of the trees its manufacture decimates. Large print is used throughout to spare your eyesight. Conservation in every area of your life is now the watchword!! My advice, therefore, will be condensed to a few fundamental principles, designed to ease your trip to the Poorhouse and to insure that you arrive in style.

Remember, it is only your money you have lost-- from this moment forward, your ATTITUDE is far more important than your bank account. At the outset, be reminded always to lower your voice in adversity. Accounts of your distress will be far less exaggerated, both to yourself and to your listener, if you speak in calm, low pitched tones. Better still, avoid referring to the recent unpleasantness at all. Bad news travels fast --- your friends have already heard the worst. Anyone who has not known Spanish people from whatever

ATTITUDE IS EVERYTHING

walk of life---for peasant and grandee have the same impeccable manners -- has missed a lesson worth learning. The Spaniard's sense of personal worth is totally unaffected by his possessions ... or lack of them. It would be unheard of for such a man to become bitter, complaining and depressed over the loss of money..Oh it very well might be mentioned to friends simply to explain why Maria Conception's coming out ball had been cancelled; but to dwell upon one's misfortunes? Never!!

Before we proceed let us consider the positive aspects of the situation. You will no longer be of interest to kidnappers, the IRS, alumni fund solicitors, confidence men, trust officers, litigation lawyers, panhandlers, grave robbers, indigent relatives and organized charities. Furthermore, you'll be spared an endless stream of invitations to organ and disease galas.. To these advantages, one might add that the chances of your children becoming hopelessly spoiled will be greatly minimized. There is an old Spanish proverb which warns, "Don't let ill fortune feel at home in your life." If ignored, laughed at, or otherwise made to feel she doesn't belong there, she'll move on. If, however, ill fortune seems determined to tarry, it is within your power simply to disregard her presence.

Remember, now and always, your brow should be serenely unlined! No matter what the problem --unpaid bills, mortgage foreclosures, bankruptcy procedures -- your expression must remain as inscrutable as that of a Japanese croupier. Facelifts are not in your budget. Rather than indulging in an endless review of your woes, reread the list of those which no longer need concern you. Count them like sheep until the panic passes. You will now be ready to think calmly and plan rationally. Worry never solved a single problem. Prayer, on the other hand, will place it all in more capable hands. Let us remember for a moment those aristocratic Russians who went from palaces in Petrograd to cold water flats in Flat Bush, without a trace of rancor. "The revolution, you know ... " airily spoken, with a debonair wave of the hand to indicate the relative unimportance of their change of address.

But be aware that no matter where you have landed, this is certainly no time to neglect your APPEARANCE. You can bet your glass slipper Cinderella wore rubber gloves when busying about the chimney hearth! And if you are accustomed to glittering do not suddenly go all dull and drab. Should your best diamonds need be sold to pay the rent, good paste will hold your image together till times improve. And certainly, any tendency to dress as though one were in mourning should be studiously avoided. Now is the time to clothe oneself in bright plumage. Our friends don't mind our being down and out half so much as our *looking* down and out. When your last faithful

retainer is no longer in service and it is you now who must answer each knock at the door, make it a rule always to greet your caller looking cheerfully composed ... even if its only a cold eyed collector from "accounts receivable," *particularly* if it's a cold-eyed collector from "accounts receivable." One hears they can be a rather testy lot. An elegant seventy year old of my acquaintance insists there is no reason why a woman shouldn't always look her best, and this one does. Due to a recent instability in the stock market, she had to give notice to butler, cook and maid, and can now be seen daily in the supermarket, walking majestically among the vegetables and soap powders as though she were inspecting the paddocks at Deauville.

"One's carriage is one's carriage," she maintains, "whether queing up at a check-out counter or waiting to be presented at court. One simply mustn't allow bad luck to take hold --- defy it immediately, no matter how overwhelming." You can still wear designer labels if you are willing to be seen in the local thrift shops. A certain second hand car vendor in the states displays a sign which asks, "Are you secure enough to drive a used car?" (Surely everyone knows by now that "second hand good" is better than "second rate new"). In a flurry to replenish your wardrobe so as to carry on with panache, never forget that the most important thing you will ever wear is the expression on your face.

ARE YOU SECURE ENOUGH???

Resentment and bitterness turn mouth corners down, give a jaundiced tinge to the complexion, and add years to your appearance.

Keep the spirit of ADVENTURE! You're now entering unchartered territory and your present financial status may lead you into interesting situations never dreamed of. A certain resourceful woman comes to mind whose quick handling of the barbs of fate turned misfortune into instant happiness. Courtney K --, at 20, was one of those incredibly beautiful American creatures who seem to suggest some other worldly species not indigenous to this planet. Skin, hair, fingernails --- all were a triumph of the optimum metabolism of protein. Add to this harbinger of certain bliss a sizeable inheritance from her maternal grandmother. What could possibly go wrong? Two disastrous marriages is what --one to a spendthrift fortune hunter who left her for a trendy morsel who manicured his nails on Tuesdays--- the other, a thoroughgoing cad who took off for Marrakesh (or was it Fiji?) with what remained of her inheritance. Our Courtney K ---, at 30, was still beautiful, but with a paucity of funds and three runny nosed children to support. (The fact of their noses running is not irrelevant; this sort of random catarrhous effusion can drive a parent up the wall even in the best of times). Ill prepared to enter the world of commerce, and totally unable to pay a suitable governess if she did, matters could have ended in the hands of a local welfare worker -- rented rooms with peeling plaster, food stamps, bare survival. Time was of the essence. Rushing to a neighborhood kiosk, Courtney K-- poured through the newspapers of all the major cities, and subsequently found a discretely worded advertisement placed by an elderly woman seeking a "refined companion." Such a charming letter of application was sent off that, despite the three children, an interview was immediately granted. On the big day all noses were carefully wiped, the small girl made a perfect curtsey, and the boys kissed the old lady's frail fingers with just the proper shade of shyness that fairly shrieks "bien eleve." By sundown the little family was happily ensconced in the west wing overlooking the orangerie. Resourceful Courtney K -- had turned bad luck into good before it had a chance to "jell." You've guessed it-- a year later, in the folly at the end of the garden (or were they seated on the ha ha?), her employer's handsome physician purposed marriage! Alas, he was unable to stop the sniffling, but a codicil in the old lady's will left the three children in linen handkerchiefs for life. Let us suppose instead that Courtney K--had *not* gotten the job and that the worst possibilities had been realized. She would still have told her children that whether they live in schloss or slum the same good manners obtain. If peeling plaster falls one simply stoops down, picks it up, and places it

THE SAME MANNERS IN SLOSS OR SLUM

without comment into some sort of container for litter. To complain would be shockingly unbecoming. Remember, "A whine is mother to a snarl "

Now, suppose you're a great sportsman -- one of the best around. You go grouse shooting in Scotland, big game hunting in Bechuanaland. Your picture was on the cover of last month's Rifle and Reel. Suddenly you haven't the price of a fishing license, and even your favorite elephant gun had to be sold to pay for groceries. Do you bemoan your lost pleasures? Do you cast sidelong, envious glances at your old companions as they set off for the bush? Indeed not! You become militantly active in the SPCA and publicly eschew your past irresponsible behavior. You talk loftily now of endangered species -- environmental protection-- man's relation to beast. Your old crowd may think you have gone around the bend, but as crusaders always hold a great attraction for women, the old crowd may end up joining you. In one such case this face saving ploy led a certain young gallant to see things from a totally new point of view, and to find in himself feelings long suppressed. Brought up in a tradition he had blindly accepted, he hunted because his father and grandfather hunted. Recently he has been actively espousing a cause he has come to believe in and has never been happier in his life. I am told a once endangered species of spotted bloat fish now bears

EVERYONE IS HAPPIER WHEN HE HAS A CAUSE

his name.

Never stop PLAYING or doing those things you most enjoy. Let us suppose the twenty room house with the olympic pool is in the hands of the receivers, and resignations from the golf club, the tennis club, the squash club et al have been tearfully tendered. Let us suppose even the weekly game of backgammon at interesting stakes must be foregone. Switch to chess. Chess is intellectually stimulating, seldom used for gambling, and commands a certain respect. Swimming, tennis and other sports can still be healthy diversions. To be sure, the YMCA is not exactly your "mallet and racquet club" of better days --- but only a snob would cavil at the change of venue. Viewing reruns at the neighborhood cinema may lack the exhilaration of attending a Broadway opening, but it is certainly preferable to sitting at home feeling sorry for oneself. The symptoms of anhedonia are listless eyes and sagging shoulders --these you can ill afford. Consider the case of Felicia M--, a newly impoverished widow with two small daughters to care for, virtually penniless and alone. She had to give up her large house, then sell the family heirlooms in order to pay her late husband's debts. Mercifully, she found gainful work in a large city in the east where she and the children soon took up housekeeping in rented rooms. Every Sunday following church, she marched the

EXERCISE IS EXERCISE,
NO MATTER THE VENUE

two little girls to a nearby museum. After visiting the old masters, they spent an hour or so in the decorative arts gallery on the second floor, and indeed, over a period of time the girls learned all there was to know about its contents. They began to think of the gallery as their second home, and raced through their catechism each Sunday in anticipation of returning.

Granted, the first time they tried to sit on a Louis Quinze fautuiel, the alarm went off --and when the younger girl picked up the Nymphenburg Satyr embracing Aphrodite, a guard fainted. But matters were soon put right and the children were allowed to continue their Sunday visits. One can easily imagine that this early exposure to the finest will influence their taste for life. I am told Felicia, herself, is now an appraiser of 18th century prints and drawings at a leading auction house. No longer able to own beautiful things, she has nevertheless contrived to be surrounded by them. Time, like money, must now be carefully spent. Don't fall into the trap of mindless escapism. This is not the moment to sit glued to those endless soap operas, intermittently interrupted by unctuous voices flogging the latest breakfast cereals or diapers for the elderly guaranteed not to leak. Don't misunderstand, modern man is fortunate that there are indeed those dedicated to the manufacture of diapers for the elderly -- and that there are means of communication through which

CONTRIVE TO BE AROUND BEAUTIFUL THINGS

their availability is made known to a wide audience. But at this stage in your affairs, you'd be best advised to turn the dratted thing off and reach for a good book. Fyodor Dostoievsky, Marcel Proust, Thomas Mann, Edith Wharton---their hardy protagonists offer valuable lessons in damage control and a proper handling of the vicissitudes of fate.

FOOD alas, so daily -- must now be carefully re-assessed. Face the fact, head-on, that rich, high caloric delicacies must go! You no longer have discretionary funds to spend on doctors, fat farms, or detoxifying spas. From now on raw vegetables and fruits should be high on your every menu.

And while you are at it, throw away the frying

pan. It will save cleaning greasy dishes and overhead oven hoods. Furthermore, the frying pan may well be implicated in cases of elevated cholesterol, incipient obesity, and gall stones. Such plagues you don't need even in prosperity. When one has the means to pay the piper, it's tempting to adopt a rather cavalier attitude vis a vis one's dining habits. Give or take an inch or two, here or there -- a good tailor can always adjust the seams. No more!! Be reminded also that you do not have the means now to splurge on cigarettes and alcohol. Besides, it is becoming increasingly fashionable not to smoke, and your wine and liquor should be saved for guests. But please guard against adopting a pious attitude in

"SOMETHING FROM THE SALAD BAR, PLEASE"

your abstinence. Just because *you* have stopped drinking doesn't mean *they* should. If, despite your enlightenment, you're still having trouble controlling the passions of the palate, spend a modest sum on an experienced hypnotist. You were not born craving crepe suzettes and vintage Lafitte Rothschild. Learned conditioning can be unlearned. Settle the matter early on -- and don't look back! The world may entertain a sort of Byzantine tolerance for the fat and rich, but for the impecunious obese--- there are few valentines. Who ever said life is fair? To be poor successfully (an oxymoron indeed, but no matter) takes an inordinate amount of self-discipline. But remember that he who conquers himself is greater than he who takes a city. Food, drink and tobacco offer you that noble opportunity.

Be advised also that you don't need a lot of fidgeting, hyperactive children revved up on junk food to spice your day. Carefully supervise their diet as well. At the same time, you might insist the little darlings turn off the hard rock and listen to classical music instead. Show them that the price of a Ninetendo game can buy balcony tickets to a thrilling symphony or even an opera. As an added bonus, the climb will provide excellent exercise. Help your children discover that trips to a nature center or an archeological museum can be more exciting than a science fiction film. Between the venus fly trap and the mummified body of a

"FRESH FRUIT, CARROTS AND SPINACH FOR SUPPER, DEARS"

Pharaoh, they can have quite an afternoon for themselves! You do want to leave them with something that is not at the mercy of Dow Jones averages or fluctuating interest rates---n'est pas? In cloudy weather expect certain of your friends to drift away ... but given this caveat, be prepared for them to drift quickly back, if and when you recoup your losses. At the same time you are now likely to attract an interesting set of *bad* weather friends. Friends who ignored you when the sun was shining now rush to your side like boy scouts looking for a good deed to perform. Your true friends who are there, rain or shine, you will now enjoy, appreciate and cherish as never before ---- and see to it that you treat them accordingly.

This brings us to the subject of HOSPITALITY which, after all, is really a state of mind. It says "I want to receive you in my house and share with you whatever I have." I am reminded of a marvelous old contessa in Rome, once so renowned as a hostess that duels were fought for an invitation to her table. The wars saw the loss of all her properties. Now in her late 80's, she lives in abject poverty, wearing shredded finery and selling off the pitiful remains of better days in order not to starve. When I first met her, she was reduced to a single room with a bunsen burner; even the telephone had been recently removed for the usual reasons. No matter, beautifully written notes were frequently sent to friends inviting them to drop in

HOSPITALITY IS A STATE OF MIND

"around 4:30 or 5:00." She would add a brief P.S. "Better bring along a pinch of your favorite tea --- tastes differ so. I'll have plenty of hot water." The silver service long gone, she served from a pottery jug. The mismated porcelain cups were badly chipped, and the crest embroidered tea napkins lay in tatters. There were seldom any accompanying sweets. Nevertheless, a sympathetic ear awaited each guest, a genuine interest in his comfort expressed. D'Anuzio's poetry was quoted, old picture albums were brought out and a great deal of laughter was shared. The old girl was literally down to her last lire, but she had not lost the spirit of hospitality.

Or consider a certain charming Venetian who has run through a series of inherited palazzos facing the Grand Canal and is still known as one of Italy's great hosts. Reduced in the end to only three rooms on the piano nobile of the last remaining property, he has never stopped giving glorious parties. Cramped for space, now treasures and junk alike are piled in a shapeless heap at one end of the drawing room, and there are no longer any liveried servants to tidy up before the guests arrive. Our innovative friend simply throws a huge piece of damask over the entire unsightly jumble, and should questions be raised, he breezily explains, "an experimental sculpture, you know, a sort of `stabile in cloth.'" No one dares pursue the subject further.

Another example is Monique de M --- , a French woman who is irresistibly delightful as

JUST CANDLES AND AFFORDABLE FLOWERS

only the French can be when they put their minds to it. The chateau in Normandy destroyed in the war, the fortunes scattered, she lives with her husband and five children in a small flat in Paris. It is simple and almost bare, nothing of any real value except a fine collection of books. "Never own what one can't maintain with ease," is her motto. Every extra franc goes toward the children's education--- the best schools, tutors for added languages, and of course, dentists to straighten teeth. There is little left for entertaining.

Yet Monique and her husband, so constantly in demand, would never dream of letting an invitation go unreciprocated. Twice a year the near empty flat is lit by candles throughout and further brightened by enormous bouquets of fresh flowers. The best champagne they can afford fills borrowed glasses as a friend's birthday, anniversary, arrival or departure is celebrated. With such blithe esprit, who needs a chateau??

On the subject of hospitality, a warning must be interjected. In an effort to carry on, we must always consider our friends' feelings, time and strength. A case in point is that of a well known London hostess who was left without a bean. (Bad investments, an unscrupulous nephew, the old

story.) In any event, suffice it to tell you that she moved from her fashionable flat in Mayfair to an attic in a building that had no lift. Bright invitations were sent out to her friends, all of a certain age, to come to the christening of her new digs. Alas, those who were not carted off in a national health ambulance during the climb arrived at the 8th floor in a state of such severe hyperventilation that no amount of thrifty little cold cuts could possibly revive them. And it is said that an ancient viscountess is still up there, unable to muster sufficient strength for the descent. One need not add that the soiree was a total disaster! Bravely refer to your inaccessible roost as a "penthouse" --- rave about the view, the quiet, the unpolluted air --- but, in all good conscience, don't ever invite anyone over 35 to sample them. Better to stand your friends to a round of schnapps at the neighborhood pub than to precipitate in their untimely demise. Remember, you are in no position to send flowers or memorial contributions, so it's better to keep your friends alive. Now for a worst care scenario. Suppose you are an able bodied male who, for whatever reason, has suddenly lost a six figure salaried job, and there appears to be little hope of securing another --- at any figure. Or imagine that you are living on inherited stocks that suddenly plummet--- shades of the Great Depression. You've never worked a day in your life. Now if things get *really* dicey and

ARTISTS ARE ALLOWED TO STARVE WITH RESPECT

it looks as though you'll never find remunerative employment --- or receive another inheritance, then for pity's sake do start writing blank verse --- or painting vague, abstract blotches on oversized canvases --- or composing music for the medieval flute. No one will understand what on earth you're about, but there is always a certain cachet surrounding artists and visionaries. Indeed these seem to be the only ones we allow to starve with any degree of respect. There is something highly compelling about a pale, obscure poet bleating out his message to the world in trembling metaphors that don't rhyme. Women literally fall at their feet longing to be an acknowledged muse. (In such a rarified atmosphere, crass money would almost seem an embarrassment). Even a penniless gargoyle will have a following if he is said to be at work on a novel or a play. He need never finish the former or have the latter produced. An image has been established nonetheless, and he can dine out for years on the mystique of authorship.

In the case of unexpected impoverishment it should be remembered that LOCATION is all important. If you were suddenly sawed off at the knees you wouldn't continue hanging out on a basketball court! If you suddenly lost your mind, you wouldn't still apply for early acceptance at MIT! By the same token, you must now carefully avoid Newport, St. Moritz, Monte Carlo, the Hamptons. *Poor in Palm Beach?? A condition*

"NO, THIS YEAR I THINK INDONESIA WILL BE MORE AMUSING"

too miserable even to contemplate!!.

To those of you who are able to scrape up the airfare, I say---- head for India! Polo is still affordable there. (Note: The inside of a banana peel is excellent for polishing boots, and of course the fruit itself is an excellent source of potassium. Waste not -- want not.) There are also smaller, highly romantic spots around the globe compatible with shrinking funds --- the Greek coast ----the islands of Indonesia--- Tangiers; and for the very young, childless and intrepid, the wilds of New Guinea offer adventure at a modest price. Be assured every respectable Book Club in the western hemisphere will beg you to lecture, if and when you ever return. Of course I suppose one can live quite cheaply in Afghanistan --- but there *are* limits.......Who knows, dear reader, you might even want to become a permanent emigré to a foreign land. There, it's possible you could discover and hone a whole new set of skills. (How many Americans owed it all to a certain potato famine in Ireland!) At the very least it will give you an alternative way of viewing the world --- and a keen awareness of how parochial and subjective our judgements are.

There we have it. And in the end, you see its all a matter of ATTITUDE. So heads up! backs straight! The telephone may ring at any minute, saying a long forgotten step-aunt has left you a tidy inheritance in woolen futures. And then

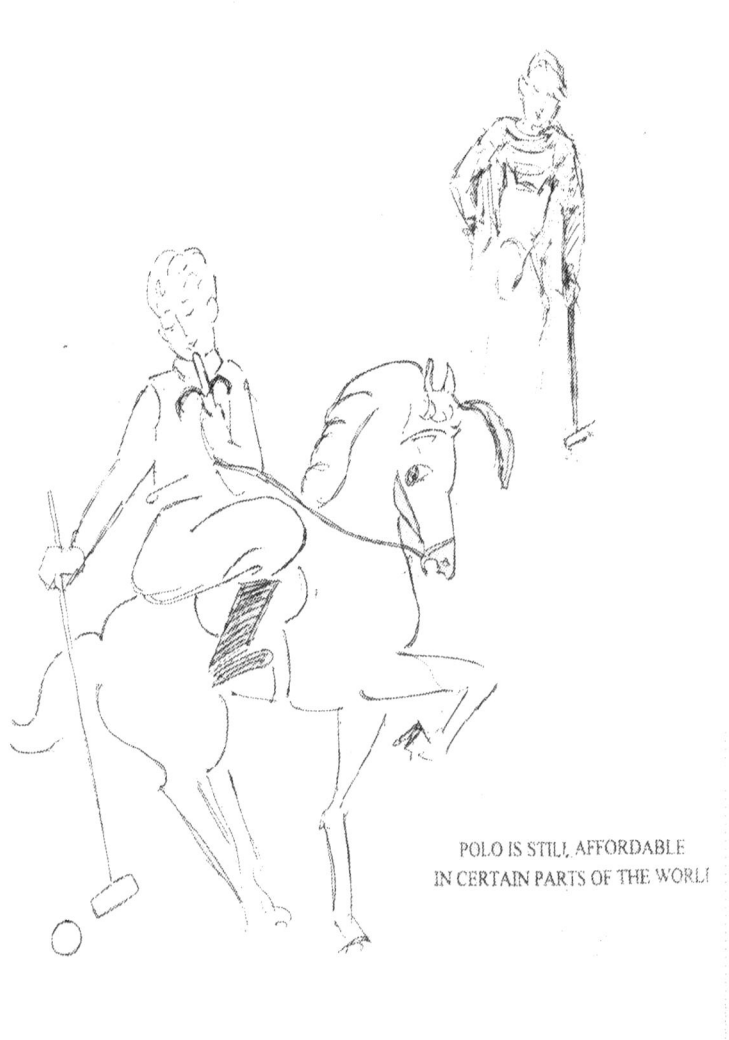

POLO IS STILL AFFORDABLE
IN CERTAIN PARTS OF THE WORLD

again ---it may not. But even so, if you have followed this advice, you will by now be more interesting, more resourceful, healthier and happier than most of your affluent peers---- and your well mannered, self-sufficient children will rise up to bless you. There could be a worse fate, believe me. BON VOYAGE,

EPILOGUE

THE READER'S OWN PERSONAL

TRAVEL LOG

Attitude

Write 30 times

I have lost only my money

(Make your entries as legible as possible. This exercise will improve your penmanship as well as your outlook.)

1

2

3

4

5

6

7

8

9

10

11

12

13

14

15

16

17

18

19

20

21

22

23

24

25

26

27

28

29

30

Composure

write 30 times

I will not frown, worry nor complain

(Smile happily as you write this)

1

2

3

4

5

6

7

8

9

10

11

12

13

14

15

16

17

18

19

20

21

22

23

24

25

26

27

28

29

30

Advantages

30 times

There are certain advantages to having less money

(OK—just do it! You are reprogramming your subconscious)

1

2

3

4

5

6

7

8

9

10

11

12

13

14

15

16

17

18

19

20

21

22

23

24

25

26

27

28

29

30

Appearance

write 30 times

I will never be seen poorly groomed nor badly dressed

(Go comb your hair before you write this)

1

2

3

4

5

6

7

8

9

10

11

12

13

14

15

16

17

18

19

20

21

22

23

24

25

26

27

28

29

30

Food

write 30 times

I will eat only healthful and non-fattening foods

(Do not smoke—or chew on your eraser as you write this)

1

2

3

4

5

6

7

8

9

10

11

12

13

14

15

16

17

18

19

20

21

22

23

24

25

26

27

28

29

30

Enjoyment

write 30 times

I will exercise, read worthwhile books, and listen to great music

(Maintain impeccable posture as you write this)

1

2

3

4

5

6

7

8

9

10

11

12

13

14

15

16

17

18

19

20

21

22

23

24

25

26

27

28

29

30

Hospitality

write 30 times

I will share with my friends whatever is left

(Try not to think about what's left' as you write this)

1

2

3

4

5

6

7

8

9

10

11

12

13

14

15

16

17

18

19

20

21

22

23

24

25

26

27

28

29

30

CAUSES

write 30 times

I will give of myself to a worthy cause

(Think of tomedoes, terrorists, and tidal waves as you write this. It will put your problems in prospective.)

1

2

3

4

5

6

7

8

9

10

11

12

13

14

15

16

17

18

19

20

21

22

23

24

25

26

27

28

29

30

Adventure

write 30 times

I will seek new opportunities and new venues

(As you write this, think of all the things you couldn't do when you were too busy making or spending money)

1

2

3

4

5

6

7

8

9

10

11

12

13

14

15

16

17

18

19

20

21

22

23

24

25

26

27

28

29

30

About the Author

Recalling the fate of the Wizard of Oz when his cover was blown, the author prefers to remain anonymous-Sages should be heard and not seen! Moreover, words of advice from unidentified sources are more likely to be acted upon as they carry the implications of universal consensus. Suffice to say, the author is of a certain age and has lived in many parts of the world.

www.ingramcontent.com/pod-product-compliance
Lightning Source LLC
Chambersburg PA
CBHW030842180526
45163CB00004B/1433